Editor: Alan White

APP

Andrew

Sunderland College

B61662

City of Sunderland College

Bede Learning Centre

This book is due for return on or before the last date shown below

3.0 JAN 2009		

Author _Boxer, Andrew_

Group ___H___   Class___940.5312___

28 day loan

CITY OF SUNDERLAND COLLEGE LIBRARY

Collins Educational

Published by CollinsEducational
An imprint of HarperCollins*Publishers*
77–85 Fulham Palace Road
London W6 8JB

© HarperCollins*Publishers* 1998

First published 1998

ISBN 0 00 327 125 0

Andrew Boxer asserts the moral right to be
identified as the author of this work.

All rights reserved. No part of this publication
may be reproduced, stored in a retrieval
system, or transmitted in any form or by any
means, electronic, mechanical, photocopying,
recording or otherwise, without either the
prior permission of the Publisher or a licence
permitting restricted copying in the United
Kingdom issued by the Copyright Licensing
Agency Ltd, 90 Tottenham Court Road,
London W1P 9HE.

**British Library Cataloguing in
Publication Data**

A catalogue record for this book is available
from the British Library.

Acknowledgements

The author and publishers would like to thank
the following for permission to reproduce
illustrations:

Solo Syndication Ltd (p27), Imperial War
Museum (pp36, 38 left), Katz Pictures/Mansell
Collection (p38 right).

Cover photograph:
Portrait of Neville Chamberlain by Sir Herbert
James Gunn (1893–1964), Carlton Club,
London, UK/Bridgeman Art Library,
London/New York.

Edited by Lucy Courtenay
Design by Derek Lee
Map by Tony Richardson
Production by Anna Pauletti

Printed and bound by
Scotprint Limited, Musselburgh

CITY OF SUNDERLAND COLLEGE
LEARNING CENTRE

ORDER NUMBER	Don
	5/02
	B61662
ACCESSIONED BY	

Contents

Introduction

The concept of appeasement

Defining appeasement

Neville Chamberlain, Britain's Prime Minister from 1937 to 1940, is the man most associated with the policy of appeasement. This is because his handling of the Czech crisis in 1938 was the most controversial example of the policy in action. Furthermore, the outbreak of war in 1939 showed that his policy had been a spectacular failure. Chamberlain himself admitted as much in his radio broadcast to the nation on 3 September announcing Britain's declaration of war: 'everything I have worked for, everything that I have believed in during my public life has crashed into ruins.'

The Conservative Party had dominated British politics in the 1930s. When the war was over, it was decisively defeated in the 1945 General Election. The nation appeared to be offering its verdict on the policy of appeasement. During the Cold War that followed, Western policy-makers wanted to show that they had learnt the lessons of the 1930s. They regularly justified their tough stance towards the USSR by referring to the failure of appeasement to stop Hitler. 'Appeasement' became a dirty word, and Chamberlain's policy in particular was seen as nothing more than the craven submission to the threat of force.

This verdict is much too simple. Taken in its most positive sense, 'appeasement' is the honourable and praiseworthy policy of putting right someone else's legitimate grievance. This is certainly how Chamberlain understood it. The governments of the 1930s were not unique in seeking to redress international problems this way. The term 'appeasement' can also be used to describe a country's attempt to use diplomacy to reduce the number of its potential enemies. This is what the politicians of the 1930s were trying to do. But in this respect also they were no different from British governments before or since.

Appeasement in context

Even if examples of 'appeasement' can be found elsewhere in British foreign policy, the 1930s remain especially controversial. Never before had Britain faced such an acute set of simultaneous problems. With its economic resources dwindling, and without the protective umbrella that NATO has provided since 1949, Britain faced three potential aggressors: Germany, Italy and Japan. Whatever response British politicians chose would be problematic. Chamberlain's faith that he could find fair solutions and keep Britain out of a costly and destructive war bitterly divided his contemporaries and has excited lively historical debate ever since.

Any appraisal of the policy of appeasement in the 1930s needs to take account of the context in which the British governments of the day were operating:

◆ Britain's economic decline was manifest but her world-wide commitments and responsibilities were, if anything, larger than they had been before the First World War.

◈ Governments had to take much more notice of public opinion because the reform acts of 1918 and 1928 had given everyone over the age of 21 the right to vote.

◆ Support from the Empire and Commonwealth could not be taken for granted.

◆ It was increasingly clear that the Treaty of Versailles, signed in 1919 after the First World War, had complicated rather than solved the problem of Britain's relations with her major European neighbours, France and Germany.

It is also important to remember that appeasement was not a single policy. It was widely accepted in the 1930s that Britain could not afford to take on all three of her potential enemies simultaneously as well as meet her obligations to the League of Nations. This left plenty of room for disagreement about what Britain's priorities should be. Different countries threatened Britain's interests at different times and in different places. Deciding on the appropriate response to each succeeding crisis involved decisions about strategic priorities and economic policy as well as diplomacy.

If the advocates of appeasement disagreed amongst themselves, so did their opponents. Churchill was a lone voice for most of the decade. The Labour Party – simultaneously demanding disarmament and greater support for the League of Nations – came close to contradicting itself. Anthony Eden, whose resignation in 1938 established his reputation as an opponent of appeasement, disagreed with Chamberlain's policy towards Italy and the United States, not with the policy of appeasement as such. Significantly, even after his resignation, Eden did not join Churchill's group of appeasement critics.

Chamberlain and appeasement

The conduct of British foreign policy changed when Chamberlain became Prime Minister in 1937. He once said of himself, 'I cannot contemplate any problem without trying to find a solution for it.' His predecessors, MacDonald and Baldwin, had been content to react to events, but Chamberlain injected a sense of purpose into foreign policy. He believed that the outstanding problems of European diplomacy could be solved and a general settlement achieved. He was a man of great energy who dominated his Cabinet and his government and was even prepared to shackle the press in pursuit of his objectives. Chamberlain loathed war and was well aware of the damage it would do to Britain's prosperity and status in the world. He also believed that the European dictators, although aggressive, were essentially realistic men. He continued to hope that they could be brought to the negotiating table to achieve their objectives long after most of his colleagues had given up hope of maintaining peace. Chamberlain's single-minded purpose explains why the policy of appeasement is inseparably linked with his name.

2 *The international context*

Britain, the Empire and Europe

Key points

◆ Britain's changing position in the world
◆ Governing the Empire
◆ The legacy of the Treaty of Versailles
◆ European international relations in the 1920s
◆ The Locarno Treaties of 1925
◆ Disarmament
◆ The impact of the Depression

Britain's changing position in the world

Britain's 19th century supremacy

In the 19th century Britain ruled the largest empire the world had ever seen. It covered a quarter of the globe. British power was unchallenged because she possessed a powerful navy and, for most of the century, was the world's leading industrial nation. There were few threats to the integrity of her overseas Empire. Japan remained a small, closed Asiatic community until late in the century, and the United States could not yet be classed as a world power. Only Russian ambitions in the Balkans and central Asia and rivalry with the French in Africa caused occasional alarm in London. In addition, Europe was at peace for most of the 19th century and Britain felt she could afford to ignore such continental quarrels as did occur. As Lord Salisbury observed, 'English policy is to float lazily downstream, occasionally putting out a diplomatic boat-hook to avoid collisions.'

Challenges to British supremacy

All this began to change in the last two decades of the 19th century because the conditions that had made British domination possible gradually disappeared. As the figures in Table 1 on page 47 show, Britain's percentage share of world manufacturing output was below that of the United States and Germany by the time the First World War started. In 1883 Britain possessed 38 battleships; the rest of the world put together had 40. Fifteen years later, Britain had 62 battleships but the rest of the world had 96.

The unification of Germany in the 1860s upset the balance of power that had kept peace on the continent since the defeat of Napoleon in 1815. German ambitions in Europe worried France and Russia, while Germany's desire to become an imperial and naval power alarmed Britain. Fear of Germany dragged Britain back into the quarrels of Europe as a reluctant partner of France and Russia in the First World War. After 1918, many in Britain hoped to see their country revert to its 19th century detachment from Europe. 'For us,' wrote Sir Robert Vansittart, a senior Foreign Office official throughout the inter-war period, 'European politics are mostly other people's feuds and grievances ... beyond a certain point, the quarrels of Europe are not our quarrels.'

Governing the Empire

The nature of the Empire

The Versailles Settlement after the First World War made the British Empire even larger than it had been in the 19th century. But the Empire was not united. There was no coherent system of government, no co-ordinated defence structure and no common economic policy. In the words of historian Michael Howard, the Empire had 'become a brontosaurus with huge, vulnerable limbs which the central nervous system had little capacity to protect, direct or control' (*The Continental Commitment*, 1972).

The Dominions

In the 19th century Britain had begun the process of transforming the Empire into the Commonwealth. In 1867 Canada was granted dominion status, which allowed her complete self-government in domestic matters although London retained control of her defence and foreign policy. Dominion status was granted to Australia in 1901, New Zealand in 1907 and South Africa in 1910. The commitment of the Dominions to the Empire remained strong, probably because most of their white settlers were recent immigrants from Britain. Their contribution to the Allied cause in the First World War was enormous. More than a million men from the Dominions served in the various theatres of war, and 140,000 of them were killed. This debt had to be acknowledged. The Statute of Westminster of 1931 granted the Dominions complete independence.

The Dominions remained well-disposed towards Britain, but they could not be relied on for unwavering support. Disagreements over trade policy surfaced at the Ottawa Conference in 1932. The Dominions were happy to see their exports entering Britain without paying tariffs, but were not prepared to extend the same privilege to industrial goods imported from Britain because they wished to develop their own industrial capacity. The most they would agree to was an increased tariff for non-British goods.

Australia and New Zealand were the most loyal of the Dominions. Britain was their principal trading partner and source of capital. For defence, they relied on Britain's oft-repeated promise to send the British fleet to the Far East when necessary. This spared them the expense of building their own armed forces. In 1939 Australia had an army of just a few thousand soldiers supplemented by a voluntary militia whose members trained for only 12 days a year. There was no air force to speak of and the navy comprised six cruisers, five First World War destroyers and two sloops.

At the Imperial Conference in May 1937, the Canadian Prime Minister suggested that public opinion in his country recommended Britain to 'leave the Germans and French to kill each other if they wanted to' but he also added that 'there would be great numbers of Canadians anxious to swim the Atlantic' to help Britain in war. All the Dominions disliked Britain's European commitments and did not want to see her drawn into another European war, but they exercised little influence over British policy. When war came in 1939, Australia, New Zealand and Canada joined Britain immediately. In South Africa, the pro-British premier had to overcome the hostility of Afrikaaners who remembered the Boer War before he could secure parliamentary approval for a declaration of war.

The Middle East

After the First World War Britain took control of Iraq, Transjordan and Palestine from the defeated Turkish Empire. Britain granted Iraq independence in 1932 but Palestine was to prove difficult and costly to govern. In 1937, Britain's proposal to divide Palestine between the indigenous Arabs and the immigrant Jews provoked an Arab revolt. At the height of the Czech crisis in the autumn of 1938, Britain had more than 20,000 troops tied down in Palestine.

Ireland

Both Catholic and Protestant Irishmen fought as volunteers in the British army during the First World War. This was remarkable because Ireland was on the verge of civil war in 1914 over Britain's plans to grant the country home rule – in effect, dominion status. In 1919 militant Catholic nationalists declared Ireland independent and set up their own government in Dublin. Three years of vicious fighting with the British authorities followed. In 1922 southern Ireland was granted dominion status as the Irish Free State. The six counties of protestant Ulster remained under British rule and Britain retained the right to use three ports in the south. Relations between the Free State and Britain were frosty principally because of the Ulster issue, and from 1932 the two countries were engaged in a tariff war. By 1938, with war in Europe looming, both sides were keen to settle their differences. The tariff war was ended and Britain gave up her right to use the three ports. This was a high price to pay for Irish neutrality because the ports would have been invaluable in the Battle of the Atlantic in the Second World War. But had Ireland been sympathetic to Nazi Germany, the consequences might have been worse.

India

Britain had been preparing India for dominion status since 1909, when Indians were allowed limited participation in the legislative process. Further concessions were granted after the First World War in which 1,200,000 Indians had served and 62,000 had died. Limited self-government was introduced in 1919 and extended in 1935. Indian nationalists were not content with these cautious measures and demanded immediate independence. Britain's attempts to contain Indian nationalism were unsuccessful – the Amritsar Massacre of 1919, in which British troops opened fire on an unarmed crowd and killed 379 people, and the frequent arrests of leaders such as Gandhi served only to enflame the situation.

The issue also threatened to divide the Conservative Party in Britain. Churchill sat on the back benches for most of the 1930s because he loathed the government's Indian policy. For him the Indians were 'humble primitives' for whom 'democracy is totally unsuited'. At times he mobilised significant support within the Conservative Party. The future of India was unresolved when war broke out in 1939, and the loyalty of India's population to Britain's cause could not be guaranteed.

The legacy of the Treaty of Versailles

Britain and the Treaty

The peace settlement at the end of the First World War appeared to give Britain everything she wanted. The German fleet – the creation of which had been largely responsible for Britain joining the war in the first place – lay scuttled at Scapa Flow. The German overseas empire was confiscated and her colonies were divided among the victorious allies. Britain's Prime Minister, David Lloyd George, successfully insisted that Britain should receive some of the reparations payments that Germany was required to make. All of this meant that when other issues arose concerning the treatment of Germany, Lloyd George tended to be magnanimous. British appeasement of Germany began at Versailles.

France and the Treaty

The French could not afford such generosity. Despite victory in 1918, they were all too conscious of their weakness. The north-eastern corner of the country had been devastated and France had lost perhaps as many as 1,500,000 dead and 700,000 wounded in the war. These losses were smaller than Germany's, but the consequences for France were more serious. Her population was only two-thirds the size of Germany's and her birth rate was stagnant. In the words of Professor Jacques Néré, 'for the French and Germans in 1919, the ratio of men of an age to bear arms was 1:2. Moreover, in the case of heavy industrial potential, even after reconstruction of the devastated French areas, the ratio was 1:4' (*The Foreign Policy of France from 1914 to 1945*, 1975). Furthermore, revolution in Russia had deprived France of the alliance that could pressure Germany from the east.

To the French it was essential that the Treaty of Versailles should permanently disable Germany's potential for aggression. French leaders hoped to detach the western bank of the Rhine from Germany and either annex it to France or create an independent buffer state. Pressure from the United States and Britain forced them to abandon these hopes. Instead, the Allies decided to keep troops on the left bank for 15 years. A zone on both sides of the river was created. This was to be permanently demilitarised – in other words, the Germans could neither fortify it nor station troops there. The French also received an Anglo-American guarantee against any unprovoked aggression by Germany. But this became worthless almost immediately because in November 1919 the American Senate, determined to have nothing more to do with Europe, refused to ratify the Treaty of Versailles.

Disagreements between Britain and France

When in May 1919 the Germans presented their objections to the Treaty,

Lloyd George was sympathetic but was unable to persuade either the Americans or the French to alter the terms. For the French, it was essential that the Treaty should be rigorously enforced to the letter. The British were already having doubts about a Treaty that they regarded as too harsh on the Germans. These worries were reinforced by the publication in 1919 of an influential book by the Cambridge economist, John Maynard Keynes, called *The Economic Consequences of the Peace*. Keynes argued that the political and economic prosperity of Europe depended on German recovery.

These tensions between Britain and France over how to treat Germany continued throughout the inter-war period. To the British, French intransigence made the Germans belligerent and uncooperative. They even believed that French cussedness over the Treaty contributed to Hitler's rise to power by making extreme nationalism more popular in Germany. To the French, the readiness of the British to revise the Treaty facilitated the revival of German power.

The League of Nations

The League of Nations was formally inaugurated in January 1920 but, without the United States, Russia or Germany, its effectiveness was limited, and responsibility for making it work fell to Britain and France. The French wanted it to act as an international policeman, but the British saw it more as a talking shop in which disputes could be discussed and resolved. This is why Britain consistently resisted French attempts to give the League more teeth. British statesmen and service chiefs were appalled at the notion of allowing foreigners to decide where and when Britain's already over-stretched military resources should be applied.

British attitudes to the League also complicated the conduct of foreign policy. Politicians were privately sceptical about what it could achieve, but they risked unpopularity with the voters if they did anything but praise it in public. The League also encouraged naïve optimism amongst those who believed its very existence absolved Britain from taking a direct part in resolving complicated international disputes, especially those in which British interests did not appear to be immediately threatened.

European international relations in the 1920s

The Ruhr invasion of 1923

In December 1922 the Germans failed to deliver a consignment of timber due to France as part of her reparations. On 11 January 1923, French and Belgian troops invaded Germany's principal industrial area, the Ruhr, in order to seize the reparations and teach the Germans a lesson. The invasion was a disaster. Strikes and passive resistance prevented the French from obtaining the goods they wanted, and caused hyper-inflation and political chaos in Germany. The British government was alarmed by French belligerence and worked hard to negotiate a settlement. This was achieved in 1924 when the Americans, in an arrangement known as the Dawes Plan, agreed to provide Germany with the loans necessary for economic recovery. France agreed to withdraw from the Ruhr and Germany resumed reparations payments.

The crisis was instructive. The French concluded that direct action did not

Figure 1
Germany and her neighbours in Europe, 1935

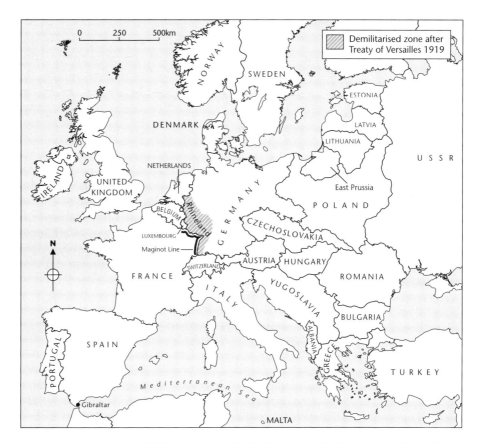

work and decided, in 1930, to secure their frontier with Germany by building a defensive fortification known as the Maginot Line. The British increasingly saw themselves as the neutral umpire in the perennial dispute between France and Germany.

The Locarno Treaties of 1925

This policy of British neutrality seemed to bear fruit the following year. The British government helped to broker an agreement between Germany and her western neighbours, France and Belgium, for the mutual acceptance of their frontiers as laid down at Versailles. The Locarno Treaties appeared to be a breakthrough in Franco-German relations because the Germans also agreed to the demilitarisation of the Rhineland. Britain and Italy agreed to act as guarantors, ensuring that all parties kept to the agreements. The following year, Germany joined the League of Nations.

The Locarno Treaties had considerable long-term significance. Nothing was said about Germany's eastern frontiers. This implied, to the Germans at least, that Britain tacitly recognised their right to change them. France gave pledges to Poland and Czechoslovakia to defend them against German aggression, thereby strengthening her commitment to eastern Europe which was to have such important consequences in the 1930s.

The Young Plan and the evacuation of the Rhineland

In 1929 a new schedule of German reparations payments was agreed that spread them over a period of 59 years. The Germans also received a new American loan. This package was known as the Young Plan. At the same time, Britain and France agreed to withdraw their occupying forces from the Rhineland in 1930 – five years ahead of schedule.

Disarmament

German disarmament

The Treaty of Versailles demanded the immediate disarmament of the defeated powers; the needs of French security required nothing less. The German army was reduced to the size necessary to guarantee internal order, a mere 100,000 men, but was not permitted tanks, heavy artillery or an air force. Her navy was reduced to being a coastal defence force. Pious statements about Allied disarmament were made at the peace conference, but nothing concrete was achieved.

The Washington and London Naval Conferences

In 1921 the Americans invited the major powers to a conference on naval limitation. The five-power treaty signed by the USA, Britain, Japan, France and Italy in December 1921 established a fixed ratio for the size of their respective fleets of capital ships (battleships and battle cruisers) of $5 : 5 : 3 : 1\frac{3}{4} : 1\frac{3}{4}$. Britain, realising that she could not afford an arms race with the United States, had signed away her naval supremacy. She also bowed to American pressure to abandon the alliance with Japan, first signed in 1902. Nationalists in Japan were outraged that their delegates had agreed to permanent inferiority, the more so when the Washington ratios were applied to cruisers as well at the London Naval Conference in 1930. For some historians, the origins of the Second World War in the Far East can be traced to Washington. 'The British, by ending the Japanese alliance, helped to strengthen those in Japan who wished to follow more chauvinistic and aggressive policies. Ties with Japan were weakened with no compensating tightening of relations with the United States' writes C.J. Bartlett (*British Foreign Policy in the Twentieth Century*, 1989). Yet it is difficult to see what realistic alternative was open to Britain.

The Disarmament Conference 1932–34

Attempts to limit the size of national armies proved even more difficult, and revived Anglo-French discord about how to treat the Germans. The French were, as ever, worried about their security, but the British believed that the inferiority imposed on Germany at Versailles could not be maintained for ever. After a good deal of stalling, the Disarmament Conference opened in Geneva on 2 February 1932. The Germans walked out in September because they had not been granted equality. Although French concessions persuaded them to return three months later, Hitler withdrew Germany permanently from both the Disarmament Conference and the League of Nations in October 1933. It became an objective of British foreign policy over the next few years to try to tempt Hitler back into the League. In 1934 the Disarmament Conference broke up without agreement.

The impact of the Depression

The Wall Street Crash and the Depression

When the American stock market crashed in October 1929, it triggered a world-wide economic depression that lasted until the mid-1930s. Thousands of American investors were ruined and so demand for goods suddenly dropped. At the end of the 1920s much economic activity in the United States had been financed by credit. This explains why the Wall Street Crash so rapidly ruined businesses and produced high unemployment. The American response was to protect her ailing industries by imposing high tariffs on imported goods. These damaged the economies of those countries that relied on exporting their goods to the United States. Exporters of primary products such as food and raw materials were particularly badly hit because the glut of the late 1920s had already forced down the price of their exports. American investors also called in their loans to Europe, which worsened the problems. This particularly affected Germany, where the fragile recovery of the 1920s had been financed by American investment.

The political impact of the Depression

The severity of the economic crisis made the system of reparations payments unworkable, and they were duly cancelled at the Lausanne conference in 1932. This concession was not enough to save the Weimar Republic in Germany. Hitler became Chancellor in January 1933 because the Depression paralysed both the German economy and its political system. Once he had established his dictatorship, he set about destroying the Versailles Settlement and re-establishing German power in Europe.

In Britain, economic problems destroyed the Labour government in 1931. A National Government was formed with sufficient electoral support to ride out the storm. But the crisis made the governments of the 1930s reluctant to spend money on rearmament in case the problems of 1931 returned.

France was unscathed at first, but by 1932 France too was in difficulties with rising unemployment and political instability. During the 1930s French politics became increasingly polarised between right and left, making a coherent national response to the threat of Germany almost impossible.

Studying the international context

1 Did the possession of a large empire make Britain strong of weak in the 1920s? Divide a piece of paper into two columns. Mark one column 'Strong' and the other 'Weak'. List your reasons in each column and compare them.

2 List the reasons why Britain felt that major war was unlikely in the 1920s. Then consider the following two questions:
♦ Were the politicians justified in their confidence?
♦ What were the major international problems of the 1920s?

3 The domestic context

Britain and appeasement

Key points

◆ The impact of the First World War
◆ Britain's fighting services
◆ Strategy and diplomacy
◆ Economic problems
◆ Popular opinion

The impact of the First World War

The war to end all wars

Britain suffered 722,000 dead and 1,676,000 wounded in the First World War. These losses were unprecedented and created a widespread feeling that carnage on such a scale should never be allowed to happen again. The war inspired a flood of literature that graphically described its horrors and reinforced public perceptions that the sacrifices of trench warfare had been futile. Modern warfare, it seemed, was so shattering and terrible that no nation could benefit from it. When the novelist H.G. Wells called it 'the war to end all wars', he believed that no-one could possibly contemplate such destruction again.

The outbreak of the war was blamed on the alliance system and the arms race. It was widely believed to have been an accidental and avoidable conflict, not the product of aggression and malevolence. This implied that future wars could be averted by disarmament and open diplomacy conducted in the League of Nations.

The wrong sort of war

Until 1914, Britain's method of fighting had remained essentially the same for two hundred years. It was the job of the Royal Navy to gain mastery of the oceans. The British Army was little more than an Imperial police force, and if fighting on the European continent was necessary, it would be done by Britain's allies whose armies might be supplemented by small contingents of British soldiers. With the brief exception of the Crimean War, no British troops had seen action in Europe since the defeat of Napoleon in 1815. This strategy allowed Britain to remain unique among the major powers in recruiting its armed forces entirely from volunteers. The total strength of the Army in 1914 (including the Regular Army, Reserves and Territorial Forces) was 733,514. This was very small by European standards.

The First World War transformed Britain's strategy. At the time of the armistice, there were 1,794,000 British soldiers serving on the Western Front alone. More than five million men served in the Army during the war, and 47% of them became casualties. The Royal Navy was reduced to a secondary supportive role, and conscription was introduced in 1916 to feed the insatiable demand for manpower. After 1918, when the wisdom of fighting in France was questioned, Britain endeavoured to return to its traditional strategy.

The Ten Year Rule

This thinking was strongly reinforced by economic realities. In August 1919 the Cabinet agreed that: 'It should be assumed… that the British Empire will not be engaged in any great war during the next ten years, and that no Expeditionary Force is required for this purpose.' This became known as the Ten Year Rule, and it justified immediate cuts in Britain's armed forces. Expenditure dropped from £692 million in 1919–20 to £115 million in 1921–22 and it did not rise again until 1934–35. Conscription was abolished in 1920, and manpower in the armed forces sank to below pre-war levels.

In 1928, the Chancellor of the Exchequer, Winston Churchill, in order to keep the spending estimates of the service ministries in check, decided that the Ten Year Rule should be annually renewed. It was only abandoned in March 1932 as a result of the Manchurian crisis but, because the Disarmament Conference was still in progress, British rearmament could not begin until 1934.

Britain's fighting services

Strategic difficulties

Between the wars there were constant arguments between Service chiefs and politicians about how best to use Britain's limited resources to defend the United Kingdom and the Empire. There were three inter-related issues:

◆ Which territories were most under threat and from whom?

◆ Was the Army, Navy or Air Force best suited to respond?

◆ How did the developing technology of warfare affect the way the armed forces should be used?

These were both strategic and diplomatic questions which became particularly hard to solve in the 1930s when Britain faced simultaneous challenges from Germany, Japan and Italy.

The RAF

The First World War created exaggerated fears of the destructive potential of air power in any future conflict. In 1922, the Committee of Imperial Defence advised that, in the next war, 'railway traffic would be disorganised, food supplies would be interrupted and it is probable that after being subjected for several weeks to the strain of such an attack the population would be so demoralised that they would insist upon an armistice.' It followed that the only way to prevent destruction was to build a bomber fleet large enough to deter an enemy attack.

The importance of bombing dominated strategic thinking about the role of air power until the late 1930s. But it did not mean that the RAF received any more money from the Treasury. The Ten Year Rule implied that there was no urgency to build a major bombing fleet, so the RAF suffered cuts along with the other two services. It was used as a cheap and effective method of policing far-flung Imperial territories.

When the government concluded in 1934 that Germany was Britain's 'ultimate potential enemy', priority was given to rebuilding the RAF as a effective deterrent. The Defence White Paper of March 1935 declared that the 'principal role' of the RAF was 'to provide for the protection of the United Kingdom and particularly London against air attack.' In the various expansion schemes produced between 1934 and 1938, priority was given to the production of bombers whose role in war would be to attack German cities in retaliation for any air assault on Britain. This strategy underpinned the government's reluctance to send the Army into Europe again – if we could bomb the Germans into submission, we would not need to send soldiers to fight them.

Strategy changed in the late 1930s. The development of the Hurricane and the Spitfire meant that Britain possessed two new monoplane fighters with the speed and manoeuvrability to shoot down bombers. At the same time, a chain of radar stations, which could detect the approach of enemy aircraft, was being built across the south and east of Britain. The Minister for the Co-ordination of Defence, Sir Thomas Inskip, challenged the bomber offensive strategy in a report presented to the Cabinet in December 1937 and suggested that priority should be given to the production of fighters. Strategy remained essentially defensive and dovetailed with Chamberlain's diplomatic objective of appeasing Germany.

Despite developing greater confidence that an enemy air assault could be warded off, British planners continued to believe that German bombers could inflict terrible losses (see Table 2 on page 47). In September 1938 the *Luftwaffe* (German air force) was thought to be capable of dropping 945 tons of bombs on England in a single day. The Air Raids Precautions department estimated that there would be 50 casualties per ton. This explains why the Ministry of Health was expecting 600,000 deaths and 1,200,000 wounded from air raids alone in the first six months of war. In fact, German bombers did not have the range to reach England until their armies captured the Low Countries and northern France in 1940, and the total number of civilian deaths in Britain during the whole of the Second World War was 60,000.

The Royal Navy

After the First World War the Navy resumed its place as Britain's principal service. Its peacetime functions were to protect Britain's sea-borne trade route and defend the territories of the Empire. But its effectiveness was progressively eroded by government financial limitations and by international treaties. At the Washington Naval Conference of 1921–22 (see also Chapter 2, page 12) the Navy had to accept equality with the Americans. Given that the likelihood of war against the USA was negligible, the Treaty at least ensured that Britain's navy was considerably larger than that of any potential rival. The Washington signatories also agreed not to build any new battleships or battle-cruisers for ten years.

At the London Naval Conference in 1930 this ban was extended for a further five years, and Britain also agreed to limitations on the rebuilding of her cruiser and destroyer fleets.

For most of the inter-war period the Royal Navy regarded Japan as its most likely potential enemy. This was welcomed by the governments of Australia and New Zealand, who relied on the British fleet to defend them. It appeared to be endorsed by the British government as well because, in response to the Manchurian crisis, the rebuilding of the base at Singapore was finally resumed in June 1932 after the postponements and delays of the 1920s. However in 1934, the threat posed by Hitler pushed Japan into second place in Britain's list of enemies.

The Navy's strategic plans met a formidable obstacle in the shape of Neville Chamberlain, who was Chancellor of the Exchequer from 1931 until 1937 and then Prime Minister. He was convinced that Britain could not afford to do anything other than ignore Japanese expansion. By 1939 Japan had slipped to third place behind Italy in the list of enemies, and the Chiefs of Staff accepted that whether or not the fleet could be sent to Singapore would 'depend on our resources and the state of the war in the European theatre'. The commitment to defend the Far East had been tacitly abandoned.

It was not just Treasury penny-pinching and government strategic priorities that weakened the Royal Navy. Its tactical thinking was somewhat conservative. Naval planners continued to underestimate the vulnerability of warships to air attack, and insufficient emphasis was given to the construction and deployment of aircraft carriers. When the war began in 1939 Britain possessed only six aircraft carriers, four of which were converted warships.

The Army

The number of territories the Army was expected to defend had increased but, after 1918, its size was rapidly cut and by 1920 there were fewer men serving than there had been ten years earlier. The government's enthusiasm for cost-cutting coincided with a widespread feeling that the commitment of a huge army to fight in France had been a terrible aberration. British people remembered the costly losses of the battles such as the Somme and Passchendaele rather than the spectacular victories of 1918. It was assumed that only generals who were insensitive, ignorant and out of touch could have sent so many men to their deaths on the Western Front. When the cartoonist David Low wanted to invent a character to be the archetypal voice of pompous, reactionary stupidity, he made him an army officer – Colonel Blimp.

To some extent the Army reinforced these negative images. Its officers continued to be drawn from a narrow upper-class social group who prized sporting rather than intellectual achievement. During the 1930s the British Army managed to squander the early lead in the use of machines and vehicles that it had established over its continental rivals. In the words of historian Edward Ranson, 'Britain entered World War Two without an effective armoured force, lacking clear ideas about tank warfare, and with vehicles with severe design and operational limits' (*British Defence Policy and Appeasement between the Wars 1919–1939*, 1993). These failings were the result partly of government financial stringency and partly of squabbles between senior officers about the role of mechanised units in modern warfare. But they were also the product of confusion about the strategic role the British Army was expected to play.

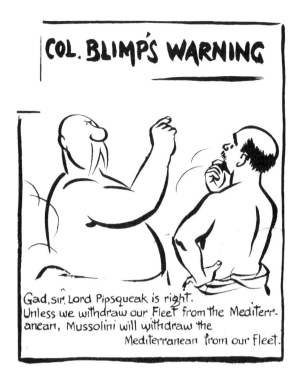

A typical David Low cartoon. Blimp's absurd comments expressed Low's frustration at the failure of Britain's rulers to develop a strong and consistent policy of opposition to the dictators.

Strategy and diplomacy

The Defence Requirements Committee

In 1922 the Cabinet told the Army that its responsibilities for the foreseeable future were home security and Imperial defence. Throughout the inter-war period there were more British troops in India than anywhere else in the Empire outside the United Kingdom. In 1933 the government established a Defence Requirements Committee (DRC) to advise on strategy and rearmament. Its first report, produced in February 1934, identified Germany as the 'ultimate potential enemy against whom our "long range" defence policy must be directed'. The DRC recommended rebuilding all three services, including the preparation of a small Expeditionary Force of the British Army to fight on the Continent. It pointed out that the Low Countries were now more vital than ever to British security, because possession of their airfields would allow German bombers to reach industrial heartlands in the Midlands and the North.

The Cabinet, dominated by the Chancellor of the Exchequer, Neville Chamberlain, disagreed. Chamberlain wanted to deter the Germans, not fight them. He insisted that priority should be given to rebuilding the bombing capability of the RAF. The notion of equipping an army to fight in Europe was dropped. The Cabinet believed that public opinion would not accept it.

Avoiding a continental commitment

The DRC reported again in November 1935. The scale and pace of German rearmament was alarming, and the Abyssinian crisis (see Chapter 4, page 28) had transformed Italy from a potential ally into a Mediterranean menace. The DRC report emphasised the fundamental problem facing British strategy and diplomacy: 'It is a cardinal requirement of our National and Imperial security that our foreign policy should be so conducted as to avoid the possible development of a situation in which we might be confronted simultaneously with the hostility of Japan in the Far East, Germany in the West, and any power on the main line of communication between the two.' The Cabinet scarcely needed reminding of this, but it reinforced Chamberlain in his hostility to the idea of preparing an Army for fighting in Europe, even though the DRC still recommended doing so. When the Arab Revolt broke out in 1937 the need to send more troops to Palestine pushed the 'continental commitment' even further into the background.

The Inskip Report, December 1937

The Minister for the Co-ordination of Defence, Sir Thomas Inskip, placed the Army firmly at the bottom of his priority list in the report he presented to the Cabinet in December 1937. He set out objectives in order of importance:

1 The security of the United Kingdom, especially from air attack.

2 The protection of imperial communications.

3 The defence of Britain's imperial territories.

4 'Co-operation in the defence of the territories of any allies Britain might have in war.' This priority could only be met when the other three had been satisfied.

The situation in 1938

The Chiefs of Staff were delighted with the Munich agreement (see Chapter 5, page 38) because it bought them a little time. Whether Britain or Germany made the better use of that time has been the subject of lively debate. The raw figures for aircraft strength (see Table 3, page 47) do not tell the whole story. In the words of historian Richard Overy, the *Luftwaffe* 'appeared numerically strong on paper but still lacked by 1938–39 much of the essential material and organisational background and [its] numbers were swollen by including transport, trainer, and converted aircraft of doubtful usefulness' (T*he Air War 1939–1945*, 1980). Michael Howard argues that, compared with 1938, Britain was able narrowly to win the Battle of Britain in 1940 because 'the effective strength of Fighter Command was nearly ten times as great and its radar installations were virtually complete' (T*he Continental Commitment*, 1972). On the other hand, Germany in 1939 was able to plunder and exploit the resources of Czechoslovakia, a country she would have been fighting against had war come a year earlier.

The continental commitment renewed

In February 1939 the British Cabinet suddenly reversed its policy. There were fears that Germany was planning an immediate assault on France. The Chiefs of Staff ruefully admitted that 'it is difficult to say how the security of the United Kingdom could be maintained if France were forced to capitulate and therefore defence of the former may have to include a share in the land defence of French territory'. The Cabinet agreed to raise an Army of thirty-two divisions to fight in Europe. The following month Chamberlain announced in Parliament that the Territorial Army would be doubled in size. Conscription followed in April. Given how late in the day the Army was told to prepare for another war to defend France, it is not surprising that it was defeated so easily by the Germans in 1940.

Economic problems

The impact of the First World War on Britain's economy

The First World War did immense damage to Britain's economy and accelerated the decline that had begun in the late 19th century. During the war Britain was less able to supply her pre-war export markets. As a result, countries either produced their own goods or bought them elsewhere. Lancashire, which before the war had dominated the world market in cotton textiles, found itself undercut by Japan and India, whose labour costs were lower. Britain's cotton exports to India declined by 53% between 1913 and 1923. Clydeside, which built a third of all the world's ships in 1913, faced post-war competition from the USA and Japan. Britain's export markets for coal were similarly devastated. The number of unemployed in Britain between the wars never fell below a million.

The First World War also saddled Britain with huge international debts. During the conflict Britain lent £1,419 million to its allies, mainly France and Russia, and borrowed £1,285 million, chiefly from the United States. After the Russian Revolution of 1917 the new communist government refused to honour the debts it had inherited from the Tsarist regime, but the Americans continued to demand repayment of the money owed to them by Britain and France. A large slice of government revenue in the post-war years was devoted to paying off Britain's war debt to the United States.

'The fourth arm of defence'

The Wall Street Crash in the United States in 1929 caused serious economic problems in Britain. Exports fell, unemployment rose to three million and, in 1931, Britain was forced to abandon the Gold Standard – a cherished symbol of the strength and stability of the pound. The politicians who dominated the National Government, which had been formed in 1931 to deal with the crisis at its worst, were haunted by the fear that rash economic policies would cause the problems to recur.

During the 1930s the Treasury maintained that Britain's economy was 'the fourth arm of defence'. They argued that, as a country dependent on imports for food and many industrial raw materials, Britain needed to maintain a healthy balance of payments. They argued that rapid rearmament would cause a balance of payments deficit because the normal pattern of trade would be upset. If factories switched to war production they would not be producing export goods but would still consume imported raw materials. Britain's balance of payments problems would cause foreign investors to sell the pound and a crisis on the scale of 1931 would recur. The Treasury nightmare was that Britain would enter a war with a weak pound and few reserves, and so would be unable to survive a major war without becoming bankrupt after a few months. Britain, it seemed, faced a dilemma. Rapid rearmament to keep pace

Chamberlain's appeasement policies

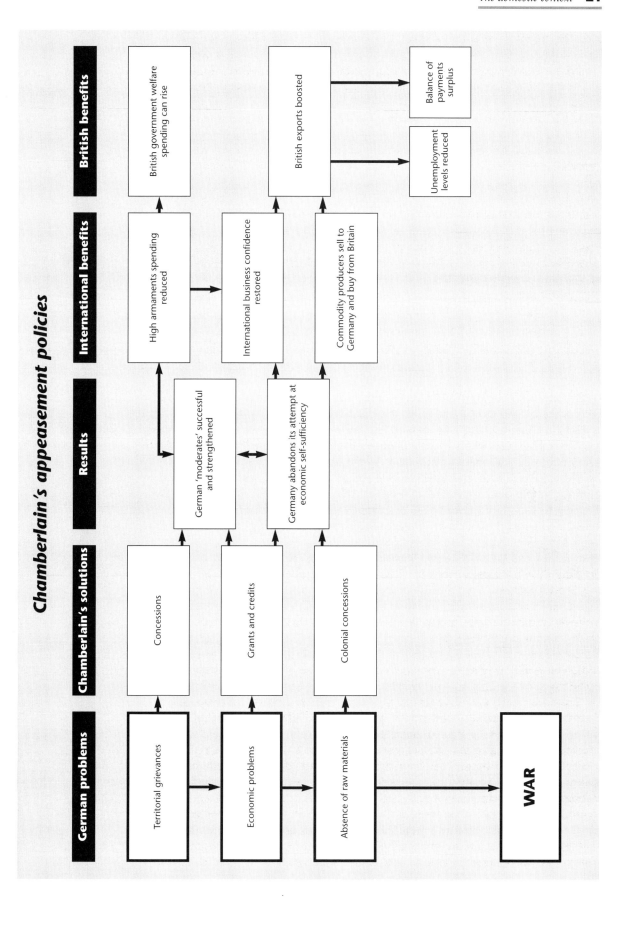

with the dictators would bankrupt the British economy. Slow rearmament, based only on what the nation could afford, might mean that the country's armed forces were not strong enough to cope with an enemy attack.

The Ten Year Rule also left an unfortunate legacy. When the government did decide to rearm, it found that the munitions industry, starved of orders since 1918, had shrunk in size and capacity. The biggest problem was the lack of skilled labour. Although there was a vast pool of unemployed workers, few of them had the skills to operate machine tools or train others in their use. The government ruled out compelling skilled workers to transfer from consumer industries to armaments factories because, as the Cabinet concluded in 1936, 'any such interference would adversely affect the general prosperity of the country and so reduce our capacity to find the necessary funds for the Service programmes. It would undoubtedly attract Parliamentary criticism.'

Economic appeasement

Treasury officials, like their Foreign Office counterparts, were keen on appeasement and believed that the government should do everything in its power to reduce the number of Britain's potential enemies. Some officials argued that economic difficulties in Germany explained why the Nazis were so aggressive. As a Foreign Office memorandum put it in January 1936, 'If … we believe that nazism is in reality a symptom and not a cause, then it is logical to deal – or at any rate attempt to deal – with it by attacking the cause itself. And what is the cause? Obviously, economic distress.'

Neville Chamberlain, who played an important part in shaping Britain's foreign policy even when he was Chancellor of the Exchequer, believed that economic policy was vitally important to the solution of Europe's diplomatic problems. He shared the Treasury view that German aggression stemmed from economic difficulties. He maintained that the Versailles Settlement, by robbing Germany of important industrial territories in Europe and her over-seas colonies, had made the Germans determined to recover them, by war if necessary. If, thought Chamberlain, British diplomacy could help to secure their return, the Germans would have no need to go to war, or even build up armaments in preparation for war.

Chamberlain and the Treasury officials were fortified in this view by a mis-taken, but understandable, interpretation of German internal politics. They believed that Hitler was receiving advice from two rival sets of advisers. One group, whom the British thought to be 'moderates', included men such as Schacht, the German Economics Minister, and was believed to share the British view of how to solve Germany's problems. The other group, designated 'extremists' by the British, was thought determined to make Germany stronger by conquest and war. Chamberlain hoped that judicious concessions to Germany would increase the power and influence of the 'moderates'. This would not only make it unnecessary for Germany to continue her preparations for war but would also reduce international tension. Even as late as February 1939, Chamberlain argued, in a speech in Birmingham, that a mutually benefi-cial Anglo-German economic agreement could help avoid recession and rising unemployment in Britain.

Unfortunately for Chamberlain, although there were 'moderates' in Germany, their influence was negligible after 1936 when Hitler demanded that the German economy should be ready for war by 1940. Schacht, who dominated German economic policy in the first years of the Third Reich, resigned from the Economics Ministry in 1937 because he could not restrain Hitler from ignoring economic realities in Germany's rapid rearmament programme. Chamberlain's mistake was to assume that Hitler was a rational leader. Economic appeasement failed because Hitler did not want to be appeased.

Popular opinion

The Franchise Act of 1918 increased the electorate from just under eight million to over 21 million, and gave women over 30 the vote for the first time. After 1928 Britain could be described as truly democratic because all men and women over the age of 21 could vote. This meant that politicians were much more conscious of public opinion in shaping their policies.

Hostility to rearmament

Finding out exactly what the public felt about foreign policy issues was difficult because the first opinion polls in Britain were not established until 1937. However, there did appear to be some widespread assumptions that politicians were reluctant to challenge. The first and most important of these was the belief that another conflict like the First World War could be avoided if the nations of Europe cut down their armaments. Spectacular evidence of this seemed to be provided by the East Fulham by-election of October 1933. The Conservative candidate, defending a majority of more than 14,000 votes, advocated rearmament. He was defeated by nearly 5,000 votes by his Labour opponent, who supported disarmament. The result had a considerable influence on the Conservative leader, Stanley Baldwin, who became convinced that rapid rearmament would mean defeat at the polls in the next general election.

Faith that the League of Nations could settle international disputes without recourse to war was another widely-held belief. At its peak in 1931 its British supporters' club – the League of Nations Union – could boast more than 400,000 members. In 1935 the Union published the result of its 'Peace Ballot' of more than 11 million people, which appeared to give a ringing endorsement of the League and its principles, including international disarmament. The rapturous reception given to Chamberlain when he returned from Munich (see Chapter 5) suggests that, even as late as September 1938, many people in Britain were anxious to avoid war and actively supported the policy of appeasement.

British domestic politics

The political landscape in Britain had been altered by the First World War. By 1922 the Labour Party had emerged to challenge the Liberals as the principal opposition to the Conservatives. The rise of the Labour Party – which had adopted an explicitly socialist constitution in 1918 – worried the Conservatives. Tory leaders believed that only moderate, unadventurous policies would be sufficiently popular to win over former Liberal voters and keep themselves in power. Defeat might deliver the nation into the hands of the wild men of the left thought to be lurking behind the leadership of the Labour Party. As it happened, similar calculations were being made by the Labour leaders, who were convinced that they could only achieve power and pick up their share of former

Liberal votes if their party adopted responsible and cautious policies. The result was a political consensus in which both main parties aimed to control the middle ground of British politics and avoid policies, particularly concerning foreign and defence issues, that courted electoral unpopularity. Winston Churchill, as Chancellor of the Exchequer in the 1920s, summed up this thinking when he opposed more money for the Navy because he could not 'conceive of any course more certain to result in a Socialist victory.'

Spending priorities

The First World War and the advent of democracy altered government spending priorities. As Table 4 on page 47 shows, expenditure on welfare took a much higher proportion of the government's budget in the 1930s than it had done in the days before the First World War. After the sacrifice of the war, the demands for extensions to the welfare responsibilities of government were irresistible. War pensions, more generous dole payments and extensions of the scope of National Insurance all added to the demands on the Exchequer in the post-war years, and no government, much less one striving to hold the middle ground, could contemplate irreversible cuts in these benefits in order to finance rearmament.

These were the domestic considerations influencing the thinking of the National Governments in the 1930s as they pondered their response to the challenges thrown at them by Japan, Italy and Germany.

Studying the domestic context

1 The three problems listed below all influenced the appeasement policies of the 1930s. Place the problems in order of importance and explain your choice:
◆ Britain's economic problems after the First World War
◆ Disputes over strategy
◆ Public opinion.

2 Which strategic decisions did the government get right in the inter-war period and what mistakes did it make? Write your answers in four sections:
◆ Decisions about the RAF
◆ Decisions about the Navy
◆ Decisions about the Army
◆ An overall assessment.

4 *Appeasement in action*

British foreign policy 1931–37

Key points

- ◆ The Japanese invasion of Manchuria in 1931
- ◆ The impact of Hitler
- ◆ Abyssinia and the Rhineland

The Japanese invasion of Manchuria in 1931

The background to the Japanese action

Japanese aggression began in the 19th century when she seized a number of islands off the Chinese mainland. Her victory over Russia in 1905 gave her not only control of Korea but also the lease from China on the Kwantung peninsula and 690 miles of the South Manchurian Railway. On the insistence of Britain and France, the Versailles Settlement sanctioned further Japanese penetration into China by transferring to Japan the German concessions in China – Kiaochow, Tsingtao and Shantung. By 1931 a quarter of a million Japanese lived in China and Japan supplied 35% of China's foreign investment. Two thirds of that sum went to the province of Manchuria, which supplied a sizeable proportion of Japan's agricultural and mining imports.

During the 1920s the Japanese population had been growing at the rate of a million a year. The country was not self-sufficient and her imported food and industrial raw materials were paid for principally by the export of raw silk, but the market for this collapsed in the Depression. Deflation and unemployment followed, encouraging the growth of Japanese nationalism and support for aggressive solutions to Japan's difficulties. The nationalists wanted to conquer Manchuria both to guarantee the imports the country needed and to provide somewhere to settle their surplus population.

Japanese aggression

On 18 September 1931 the Japanese army blew up a small section of the South Manchurian Railway near the town of Mukden. The incident was blamed on the Chinese. The army then seized the entire province, brushing aside the reservations of its own government in Tokyo. The conquest was completed early the following year and was universally popular in Japan. On 18 February 1932 the Japanese declared that Manchuria, renamed Manchukuo, had become an independent state with the deposed Chinese emperor Pu-Yi at its head.

The British response

Japan's action coincided with serious economic crisis in Britain and the formation of a National Government in August 1931. The new government's deflationary measures included wage cuts for public servants and the armed forces, and led to unrest in September among the sailors stationed at Invergordon in the Cromarty Firth. Even without these difficulties, the fleet would have been unable to offer effective resistance to Japan, as historian Christopher Thorne explains:

> 'Singapore was the key and, like the fleet's oil reserves, it bore the marks of repeated government economies. Work on the base, first authorised in 1921, had been abandoned and restarted in 1924, slowed down in 1928, slowed down and suspended where possible in 1929 and deferred again in 1930 … [In 1931] its floating dock and oil-fuel reserves lay open to attack, even from seaward … Anti-submarine and other seaward defences were virtually non-existent … Yet unless Singapore could be held intact during the 38 days that it was estimated it would take the main fleet to arrive … [Britain's capital ships] could not advance beyond India. This was recognised in the Admiralty, where it was also calculated that the Japanese fleet could be off Singapore in 10 days and then destroy the base facilities and oil supplies at its leisure' (T*he Limits of Foreign Policy, 1972*).

The government's reluctance to act was reinforced by fear that the alternative to Japanese rule in Manchuria was a Russian take-over of the province. Nor were the Americans much help. The President protested angrily but, because Britain and the United States were rivals for influence in the Far East, a co-ordinated response was impossible.

The League of Nations and the Manchurian crisis

Britain could not simply acquiesce in the Japanese take-over of Manchuria because on 21 September 1931 China appealed to the League of Nations. On 10 December 1931 the League appointed a commission of enquiry, headed by the British peer, Lord Lytton, which reported in October 1932. The Lytton Report condemned the Japanese aggression of September 1931 and claimed that Manchukuo was not an independent state. However, it also recommended that Manchuria should be an autonomous region under Chinese sovereignty with 'a substantial proportion' of Japanese advisers, and that Japanese economic interests in the area should be recognised. In February 1933, as the League voted to adopt the Lytton Report, the Japanese army invaded the Chinese province of Jehol, claiming that the region was an a integral part of Manchukuo. A month later Japan announced its withdrawal from the League.

Reactions to the crisis

Supporters of the League in Britain were disappointed that it had been unable to influence Japan, but few wanted military action. The Cabinet reluctantly concluded that British rearmament was now essential and cancelled the Ten Year Rule on 23 March 1932, but added the warning that this did not justify 'an expanding expenditure by the Defence Services without regard to the very serious financial and economic situation which still obtains'.

The impact of Hitler

Hitler as Chancellor

There was little alarm in Britain when Hitler became German Chancellor in January 1933. The *Daily Mail* even rejoiced that Germany had 'a stable government at last' and welcomed Hitler, with his 'good looks and charming personality', taking on 'the mantle of Bismarck'.

In speeches and interviews during 1933, Hitler stressed his peaceful ambitions and emphasised his desire, first expressed in his autobiography *Mein Kampf*, for an understanding with Britain. The British government responded cautiously. While anxious to reach agreement with Hitler, they were exasperated by his behaviour. Soon the evidence of German rearmament in defiance of the Treaty of Versailles was plentiful, and in July 1934 the murder by Austrian Nazis of Chancellor Dollfuss briefly excited fears of a German invasion of Austria.

The Stresa Front, April 1935

German rearmament in defiance of the Treaty of Versailles became public knowledge when, on successive Saturdays in March 1935, Hitler announced the existence of the *Luftwaffe* and the reintroduction of conscription. This alarmed Italy, France and Britain so much that their heads of government and foreign secretaries met, on Mussolini's invitation, at Stresa in Italy. The Stresa Conference produced an impressive declaration that the three powers would 'act in close and cordial collaboration' to oppose 'any unilateral repudiation of treaties which may endanger the peace of Europe'.

But the unity of Stresa was bogus. None of the three was prepared to act without the support of the others, and there were plenty of issues to divide them. Mussolini was already moving troops through the Suez Canal in preparation for his invasion of Abyssinia in the autumn. The lack of any British protest led him to believe that he had tacit approval for his invasion. He had already secured the secret support of the French, who were anxious to keep him as an ally against Hitler. The British Cabinet had agreed, before the conference began, 'to take no action [against Germany] except to threaten her.'

The Anglo-German Naval Agreement, June 1935

The emptiness of the Stresa declaration became apparent two months later when Britain signed her bilateral Naval Agreement with Germany. Without prior consultation with France or Italy, Britain agreed to allow the Germans to build a fleet of up to 35% of the size of the Royal Navy. The decision to sign the agreement was influenced by memories of the naval arms race with Germany which had dragged Britain into war in 1914 and by the anxiety of the British government to secure Hitler's signature to a treaty limiting the build-up of armaments. The Royal Navy was delighted with the agreement because, with the threat in the North Sea reduced, it could concentrate on the Far East.

Abyssinia and the Rhineland

Britain's reaction to the Italian invasion of Abyssinia

In October 1935 Mussolini launched his long-planned invasion of Abyssinia (also known as Ethiopia). His action compounded Britain's difficulties. Hard-headed realism suggested that Britain should ignore his action to maintain the Stresa Front against a resurgent Germany. The First Sea Lord, Admiral Chatfield, did not want to risk ships that he could otherwise send to Singapore if a crisis arose in the Far East. One of Britain's senior soldiers confided to his diary, 'I firmly believe that we are not prepared, morally and psychologically, for war against Italy and care very little for "poor little Ethiopia". Black races to an Englishman are always niggers and we don't see why we should be plunged into war on their account.'

More liberal-minded Britons sympathised with the plight of the Abyssinians, especially when their deposed emperor, Haile Selassie, made a dignified appeal for support in the League of Nations. After the League's shortcomings over Manchuria, the government believed that public opinion would not allow another failure. With a general election due before October 1936 at the latest, a firm stance seemed essential.

The new Foreign Secretary, Samuel Hoare, had already committed Britain. On 11 September he had told the League Assembly: 'The League stands, and my country stands with it, for the collective maintenance of the Covenant in its entirety, and particularly for steady and collective resistance to all acts of unprovoked aggression.' The government hoped that it would not have to act on these fine words. They believed that the French, who wanted to keep Mussolini as an ally, would prevent the League from taking strong action.

The League of Nations and sanctions

But sanctions were imposed. They came into force on 18 November and included a ban on imports and the export of weapons, supplies, rubber and metallic ores to and from Italy, as well as a prohibition on loans. Oil was not included because most of it came to Italy from countries outside the League. The idea was to impose sanctions which could be immediately implemented before discussing the oil sanction with the non-League suppliers. This firm action contributed to the government's resounding win in the British general election which the Prime Minister, Stanley Baldwin, called in November.

The League had also established a committee, led by Britain and France, to pursue a negotiated settlement. British diplomats had been discussing a number of boundary disputes with Haile Selassie since 1932 and, before the invasion, the Emperor had signalled his willingness to trade territory with both Britain and Italy. Mussolini's envoys in London indicated that the Italian dictator was also prepared to be flexible. His conquest was far from complete (not even the Italians thought they could win before the summer of 1937) and it seemed that a negotiated solution might be possible.

The Hoare–Laval Pact, December 1935

Sir Samuel Hoare travelled to Paris for talks on 7–8 December with Pierre Laval, who was both Prime Minister and Foreign Secretary of France. They discussed

the oil sanction. Both were concerned that Mussolini might regard it as a declaration of war, and Hoare feared some 'mad dog' act by the Italian dictator,
'directed against the British fleet or against Egypt'. Laval promised French
support for Britain in such an event, but this made him all the more anxious to
find a territorial settlement that would appease Italy. The two men concocted a
plan by which Italy would retain what she had conquered already and acquire
about a third of the rest of Abyssinia.

Unfortunately for the two politicians, the details of their plan were leaked to
the press, by which time Hoare had travelled on to Switzerland for a skating
holiday where he fell and broke his nose. In London, Baldwin responded lamely
to MPs who were angry at the government's betrayal of the principle of collective
security which it had warmly endorsed in the election campaign. Hoare resigned
and was replaced as Foreign Secretary by Anthony Eden. Laval also resigned
early in the new year.

On 26 February 1936, the British Cabinet, in an attempt to restore some of
its tattered prestige, decided to support the oil sanction, provided the
French agreed. But the new French government wanted a British guarantee
to resist any German action in the demilitarised Rhineland. This was completely unacceptable to the British, and so the oil sanction was forgotten.
The Italians made surprisingly rapid progress in Abyssinia and, by May 1936,
had captured Addis Ababa. The Emperor and his family fled, rescued from
the French port of Djibouti by a British cruiser. On 10 June Neville
Chamberlain, whose thinking was influenced by the impact that renewed
trade might have on British unemployment, described the continuation of
sanctions as 'the very midsummer of madness'. A week later sanctions were
withdrawn.

The Rhineland crisis

On 7 March 1936, Hitler took advantage of the Abyssinian crisis and marched
about 10,000 troops into the demilitarised Rhineland zone. Shortly after the
troops moved in, Hitler suggested that he was interested in negotiating new
security pacts with his neighbours and was even contemplating a return to the
League of Nations. This was a ploy to encourage Britain to restrain the French
from opposing the German actions.

Hitler's offers merely reinforced the decisions that the governments of
Britain and France had already made. The French would make no move
without British backing. The British position was summed up by Baldwin when
he told the Cabinet on 11 March that forceful action in the Rhineland would
succeed 'only in letting loose another great war in Europe'. Ministers comfort-
ed themselves with the thought that without Italian co-operation, they were
absolved from their duty to uphold the Locarno Treaties. They also knew that
public opinion in Britain would not support any action to remove German
troops from German territory.

The Spanish Civil War, 1936–39

In July 1936 the Spanish army, led by the right-wing General Franco, began a
revolt against the socialist government of the Spanish Republic. The ensuing
war became an ideological battleground between left and right in Europe. The
Republican government received some assistance from the USSR and from the
International Brigades, made up of left-wing volunteers from countries all over

Europe. Franco's Nationalists were helped by the Germans (most notoriously in the bombing of Guernica in 1937) but principally by the Italians who supplied 50,000 troops.

Hitler was delighted with the war because it drew Mussolini's attention away from central Europe and increased the chances of a clash between the Italians and Britain and France. Britain insisted on non-intervention. Although the Spanish Civil War generated great passion in Britain in the 1930s, it did not influence government policy.

Assessment

The record of British foreign policy in this period looks grim. The failure to resist aggression in Manchuria and Abyssinia encouraged the dictators and destroyed the credibility of the League of Nations. Italy was alienated as a potential ally. Aggression in Spain and China was ignored. Britain acquiesced in Hitler's destruction of the military clauses of the Treaty of Versailles without gaining much in return. Significant differences developed between Britain and France about how to handle the dictators.

There were, however, mitigating factors. Britain could not defend all the territories of the Empire, and support the French in Europe, if faced with simultaneous threats from Japan, Germany and Italy. Nor was it certain that Germany would simply have withdrawn from the Rhineland had the French been encouraged to push them out. British public opinion, which appeared to want decisive action to stop aggression but without the use of armed forces, served to complicate the issues.

The government seemed to be caught off-guard by each succeeding crisis, and struggled to formulate a coherent and consistent strategy. Chamberlain, when he became premier, was determined to inject more vigour and purpose into the conduct of foreign policy.

Studying appeasement in action

1 Do you agree with the way that foreign policy was handled in this period? What alternative policies might the government have considered or carried out?

2 Allocate the roles listed below to one (or more) of the members of your class. Hold a Cabinet meeting to decide on how Britain should react to the Italian invasion of Abyssinia. You may need to re-read Chapter 3 to remind yourselves of the strategic debates:
♦ Prime Minister (who chairs the meeting)
♦ Chancellor of the Exchequer
♦ Foreign Secretary
♦ Dominions Secretary
♦ Service ministers (Admiralty, War Office, Air Ministry).
You may wish to add ministers responsible for domestic issues such as housing, education, employment etc.

5 Chamberlain and appeasement

British foreign policy, 1937–39

Key points

◆ Chamberlain and the conduct of foreign policy
◆ The crisis over the Sudetenland of Czechoslovakia
◆ The aftermath of Munich
◆ The Polish crisis and the outbreak of war
◆ Why did Britain go to war in 1939?

Chamberlain and the conduct of foreign policy

Chamberlain's aims

Neville Chamberlain became Prime Minister in May 1937, determined to make British foreign policy more dynamic. Becoming premier allowed him to pursue his long-cherished scheme for what he called a 'general settlement' of Europe's outstanding diplomatic problems.

Chamberlain recognised that Hitler's Germany posed the biggest threat to European peace. He did not like the Nazis and realised that diplomacy needed to be backed by strength. In March 1938 he observed: 'force is the only argument Germany understands.' He described Hitler as narrow-minded and 'violently prejudiced' but believed, even as late as July 1939, that Hitler 'is not such a fool as some hysterical people make out and that he would not be sorry to compromise if he could do so without what he would feel to be humiliation'. Chamberlain was convinced that, however ghastly Hitler and the Nazis were, they were sensible enough to realise that risking war was more foolish than achieving their aims by peaceful negotiation.

To Chamberlain there were three outstanding problems:

◆ If German colonies were returned, her economic difficulties would be eased. This might encourage the Germans to slow down the pace of their rearmament and develop their trading links with Britain to the benefit of both countries.

◆ Secondly, he wanted Germany to sign an air pact comparable to the Anglo-German Naval Agreement of 1935 (see Chapter 4, page 27). This would reduce the danger of either country being devastated by bombing.

◆ Finally, Chamberlain believed that Germany had legitimate territorial grievances in eastern Europe. As he wrote to his sister six months after becoming premier: 'I don't see why we shouldn't say to Germany, "give us satisfactory assurances that you won't use force to deal with the Austrians and Czechoslovakians, and we will give you similar assurances that we won't use force to prevent the changes you want, if you can get them by peaceful means."'

Britain's potential allies

Chamberlain had firm views about the other nations of Europe. He knew that he had to keep British policy in step with French, but he didn't want to make any firm guarantees to France in case a promise of British support made them belligerent towards Germany. He did not trust the USSR and did not welcome them as potential allies. In common with many Conservatives, he regarded Communism and Fascism as equally undesirable and feared that the aim of Stalin's policy was to provoke a quarrel between Germany and the western democracies. After the Red Army was purged by Stalin in 1937, Chamberlain shared the widely accepted view that its military value was limited. He had much greater hopes of Italy. Chamberlain placed considerable faith in Mussolini's ability to restrain Hitler and spent much of his premiership courting the Italian leader.

Chamberlain knew that he would not get much practical assistance from the United States. However sympathetic the President, Franklin Roosevelt, might be to the cause of democracy, the Neutrality Acts of the 1930s prevented him from giving help to any foreign country involved in war.

Chamberlain's conduct of foreign policy

Chamberlain, in common with a number of other British Prime Ministers, wanted to run foreign policy himself and, at times, ignored or bypassed the Foreign Office. He relied heavily on personal advisers, principally Sir Horace Wilson, a civil servant who had worked in the Ministry of Labour and the Treasury. Chamberlain respected Wilson's skills as a patient negotiator who had successfully resolved a number of tricky industrial disputes. The premier disagreed with Sir Robert Vansittart, who had been the principal civil servant at the Foreign Office since 1930, about how far Germany should be appeased. Early in 1938, Vansittart was pushed aside and given the seemingly impressive but meaningless title of Chief Diplomatic Adviser.

Halifax's visit to Hitler, November 1937

In November 1937 Chamberlain irritated his Foreign Secretary, Anthony Eden, when he sent Lord Halifax rather than Eden to negotiate with Hitler. Halifax nearly caused a diplomatic incident. When he arrived at Hitler's mountain retreat he mistook the German *Führer* for a servant and almost handed him his hat and coat. Halifax faithfully conveyed Chamberlain's thinking to Hitler. The British wanted 'a lasting European peace' negotiated by Britain, Germany, France and Italy. This 'general settlement' could include the return of German colonies and Britain would not object to 'alterations in the European order' in Danzig, Austria and Czechoslovakia provided that they were achieved peacefully. When he returned to London, Halifax reassured the Cabinet that 'the

Germans had no policy of immediate adventure' but he expected the Germans to show 'a beaver-like persistence in pressing their claims in Central Europe, but not in a form to give others cause ... to interfere'. Halifax's visit fortified Chamberlain in his belief that a 'general settlement' could be achieved.

Eden's resignation, February 1938

Chamberlain's determination to conduct foreign policy himself caused the resignation of his Foreign Secretary early in 1938. When Roosevelt suggested a world conference to discuss disarmament and international relations, Chamberlain was dismissive of the idea. He sent a cool response without even bothering to tell Eden, who was on holiday at the time. Eden was annoyed because he thought that American initiatives should be encouraged. The two men also disagreed about Italy. For Eden, Mussolini was a 'complete gangster' whose 'pledged word means nothing'. Chamberlain was convinced that British friendship with Italy was essential. When Eden resigned on 20 February, Chamberlain replaced him with Lord Halifax, whose views at that time almost exactly coincided with his own.

The German Anschluss with Austria, March 1938

German troops marched into Austria on 12 March. The Austrian government had already been intimidated into offering no resistance and, on the following day, Austria was incorporated into the German Reich. Chamberlain did not object in principle to the union of Germany and Austria since both were German-speaking nations and there was plenty of evidence that many Austrians welcomed it, but he was upset by the Nazis' use of force. However, as he told the Foreign Policy Committee of the Cabinet on 15 March, 'he did not think anything that had happened should cause the government to alter their present policy, on the contrary, recent events had confirmed him in his opinion that the policy was the right one'.

The crisis over the Sudetenland of Czechoslovakia

The problem of the Sudetenland

It was clear to everyone that the next crisis would be over Czechoslovakia, because Hitler had begun making inflammatory speeches about it even before the *Anschluss*. The Sudetenland gave him a perfect excuse for making trouble. The Versailles Conference of 1919, in determining the boundaries of the new states of central and eastern Europe, had included this predominantly German-speaking region within the borders of Czechoslovakia. The three million Germans who lived there were citizens of the former Austro-Hungarian Empire, not of the Kaiser's Germany. The Czech claim to the area had been upheld at Versailles because its mineral resources and mountain defences made it vital to the prosperity and security of the new state.

The Germans of the Sudetenland presented few problems in the 1920s but, when the Great Depression of the early 1930s caused high unemployment throughout Europe, their sense of grievance grew. They regarded themselves as the victims of Czech discrimination and looked enviously across the border where, from 1933 onwards, the Nazi regime was curing unemployment and restoring German strength. In 1933, a former PE teacher called Konrad Henlein established a Sudeten German Party demanding self-government for the region. From 1935 he was being subsidised by the German government. After the *Anschluss*, the agitation of the Sudeten Germans to 'return home to the Reich' became noisy and sometimes violent.

Hitler's aims

Hitler, of course, was not really interested in the grievances of the Sudeten Germans. They merely provided him with a useful weapon with which to pursue his larger goal: the destruction of the Czech state. As a multi-national Slav democracy which had been created by the hated Versailles Settlement, the very existence of Czechoslovakia was offensive in his eyes. It was also an obstacle to his strategic plans because the German–Czech frontier, with its natural defences, was the key to mastery of central Europe. Czechoslovakia's alliances with France and the USSR made her, in Hitler's words, 'the aircraft carrier in the heart of Germany'. But he had to tread warily. Hitler was not ready for a major European war in 1938 and so, initially at least, he was reluctant to use force against Czechoslovakia. At the end of March he summoned Henlein to Berlin and told him to continue making trouble for the Czech government. Henlein summed up his instructions: 'we must always demand so much that we cannot be satisfied.' This, Hitler hoped, would encourage the British and French to abandon Czechoslovakia. He believed, as he had told his top military advisers in November 1937, 'that almost certainly Britain, and probably France as well, had already tacitly written off the Czechs and were reconciled to the fact that this question would be cleared up in due course by Germany'.

British attitudes to Czechoslovakia and the Sudetenland

Hitler's assessment of the British was not far wrong; they were extremely reluctant to risk war to prevent Sudeten Germans from joining Germany. Chamberlain took Hitler's demand for the Sudetenland at face value because he believed that Hitler wanted no more than the unity of all German-speaking peoples. In May 1938 Konrad Henlein visited London and impressed the officials he met. Vansittart described him as a 'wise and reasonable man'. The visit made the British feel that it was the Czechs who were being unreasonable.

This view was reinforced by the messages received from the British ambassador in Berlin, Sir Nevile Henderson, whose sympathies were clearly with the Germans. Henderson was influential because his views coincided with those of Chamberlain. He passionately believed that European peace could be saved only by meeting German grievances. Such concessions would strengthen the position of the supposedly moderate influences (amongst whom he numbered Göring) around Hitler. Henderson disliked the Czechs and described their president, Eduard Benes, as 'a small man' and 'pig-headed'.

Henderson's views were supported by the attitude of the British Minister in Prague, Basil Newton. He believed that Czechoslovakia, because of its mixture of nationalities, was an artificial creation that would probably not survive even without German pressure. It would be futile for Britain to go to war to defend it. The ambassador in Paris, Sir Eric Phipps, who had also served in Berlin, sent back a stream of gloomy messages about French morale, while Lord Perth in Rome reinforced Chamberlain's assumption that good relations with Italy could be restored.

The Weekend Crisis, May 1938

On Friday 20 May 1938 rumours began to circulate of German military preparations near the Czech border. Early the following day the Czech government responded by ordering a partial mobilisation, and Britain and France sent warnings to Germany. As the initial rumours were false, Hitler found himself in the unusual position of telling the truth when he denied that Germany had been preparing to attack Czechoslovakia.

The crisis had important consequences. Hitler felt humiliated and told his generals: 'It is my unalterable decision to smash Czechoslovakia by military action in the near future.' The British government were alarmed at how close they had been to war and redoubled their efforts to secure a peaceful settlement.

On 22 May Halifax, despite what he had said to the Germans two days earlier, warned the French government that they should not count on Britain to 'take joint military action with them to preserve Czechoslovakia against German aggression'. He did not want the French to assume from the outcome of the Weekend Crisis that threats were the best way to deal with Germany. As well as holding the French in check, the British put pressure on the Czechs to meet German grievances over the Sudetenland.

The Runciman mission, August 1938

Early in August Chamberlain dispatched a former Cabinet minister, Lord Runciman, to Prague as a mediator. Runciman spent a month in Czechoslovakia but his mission achieved nothing. The Czech president, Eduard Benes, was prepared to grant self-government to the Sudetenland but Henlein was uncooperative. Acting on instructions from Berlin, the Sudeten Germans increased their violence to provide Hitler with an excuse to invade. German military preparations were stepped up and the Nazi press campaign against Czechoslovakia became increasingly hysterical.

Chamberlain's decision to visit Hitler

Hitler's inflammatory speech at the annual Nazi rally in Nuremberg on 12 September was followed by further rioting in the Sudetenland. The Czech government responded by declaring martial law, and Henderson warned that Hitler was about to attack. Chamberlain decided to intervene personally.

The Berchtesgaden meeting, 15 September 1938

Chamberlain flew to Germany and met Hitler at his mountain retreat in Bavaria. They agreed that the Sudeten German areas of Czechoslovakia should be transferred to Germany. Both men were delighted. Hitler believed that Chamberlain would be unable to persuade Benes to give up the

Sudetenland to Germany, whereupon he expected Britain and France to abandon Czechoslovakia. This would allow him to enjoy a short, victorious war of conquest. Chamberlain, having secured Hitler's promise that Germany had 'no further territorial demands', believed that he could secure a peaceful resolution of the crisis.

A few days later, Chamberlain wrote to his sister about the impression he felt he had made on Hitler. 'Various people who were with Hitler after my interview [reported] that he had been very favourably impressed. I have had a conversation with a man, he said, and one with whom I can do business and he liked the rapidity with which I had grasped the essentials. In short, I had established a certain confidence, which was my aim, and on my side, in spite of the hardness and ruthlessness I thought I saw in his face, I got the impression that here was a man who could be relied on when he had given his word.'

On Sunday 18 September senior members of the French government flew to London and agreed to Chamberlain's proposals for resolving the crisis. The Prime Minister secured the unanimous consent of his Cabinet the same day. Those areas of Czechoslovakia in which the population was more than half German would be ceded to Germany. Britain and France would jointly guarantee Czechoslovakia's new frontiers. The Czechs agreed to the terms only after two days of persuasion, during which they were told that Britain and France would not come to their aid if they refused.

The Godesberg meeting, 22–23 September 1938

The day after receiving news of the capitulation of the Czechs, Chamberlain flew to Godesberg, on the Rhine, to tell Hitler the good news personally. Hitler was furious. He wanted an excuse for war against Czechoslovakia, not the peaceful transfer of the Sudetenland. He raised the stakes and demanded that Hungarian and Polish claims on Czech territory should be met and that German troops should be permitted to occupy the Sudetenland on 28 September. Chamberlain was despondent. He met Hitler again the following day, but the only concession Hitler was prepared to make was a delay of two days before German troops marched in.

Summit diplomacy was unusual in the 1930s. Chamberlain's willingness to fly to Germany showed how anxious he was to secure a peaceful outcome to the Sudeten crisis.

Chamberlain returned to London on Saturday 24 September and reported to the British Cabinet the same afternoon. He remained convinced that 'Hitler was extremely anxious to secure the friendship of Great Britain ... and that the object of his policy was racial unity and not the domination of Europe'. Chamberlain told the Cabinet that he 'thought that he had now established an influence over Herr Hitler, and that the latter trusted him and was willing to work with him'. For Chamberlain, even the Godesberg terms offered 'a wonderful opportunity to put an end to the horrible nightmare of the present armaments race'. At the Cabinet meeting the next day, Halifax dissented and said that Britain could not accept Hitler's new demands. He had already warned Chamberlain by telephone when the premier was in Germany that the 'great mass of public opinion seems to be hardening in the sense of feeling that we have gone to the limit of concession'. When the French leaders arrived in London later the same day, they, like Halifax, were reluctant to give in.

In response to Cabinet criticisms, Chamberlain sent Sir Horace Wilson, his most trusted adviser, to Berlin. Hitler told Wilson that Czechoslovakia would be smashed unless the demands he had made at Godesberg were met. Wilson reported back to the Cabinet on 27 September and recommended capitulation to Hitler. Chamberlain agreed, but opposition from Halifax and Duff Cooper, the First Lord of the Admiralty, forced him to give way.

War looked certain. Hitler had demanded acceptance of his terms by 2pm on Wednesday 28 September. The Czechs had rejected them and the French had announced that they would support Czechoslovakia. Chamberlain broadcast to the nation on the radio that evening. 'How horrible, fantastic, incredible it is that we should be digging trenches and trying on gas masks here because of a quarrel in a far-away country between people of whom we know nothing. War is a fearful thing, and we must be very clear, before we embark on it, that it is really the great issues that are at stake.' Chamberlain was convinced that the transfer of the Sudetenland to Germany, which had been accepted in principle by the Czechs, was not a 'great issue'. He ended his broadcast by promising 'to work for peace to the last moment'.

The Munich Conference, 29–30 September 1938

It was while Chamberlain was addressing the House of Commons during the afternoon of 28 September that news arrived of a last-minute reprieve. The Italian dictator, Mussolini, had responded to British requests for mediation and had persuaded Hitler to summon a conference at Munich. There was euphoria in the Commons, particularly among Chamberlain's supporters on the Tory back benches.

The following morning the entire Cabinet went with Chamberlain to the airport to see him off. The Munich Conference was attended by Hitler, Mussolini, Chamberlain and Daladier, the French Prime Minister. Neither the Czechs nor the Russians (who, like the French, had an alliance with Czechoslovakia) were invited. The terms agreed differed little in substance from those that Hitler had demanded at Godesberg. The German occupation of the Sudetenland would take place over 10 days rather than being completed on 1 October. Plebiscites were to be held in disputed areas and supervised by an international commission which would determine the new frontiers. Czechs were to be permitted to leave, and Germans to join, the transferred territories. Not surprisingly, neither the plebiscites nor the population transfers occurred.

The declaration signed by Hitler which Chamberlain read to the crowds at Heston Airport.

In the early hours of 30 September, Chamberlain had a private meeting with Hitler and asked him to sign a piece of paper he had prepared. It stressed 'the desire of our two peoples never to go to war with one another again' and promised continued joint efforts 'to assure the peace of Europe'. When he returned to Britain, Chamberlain read this declaration to the cheering crowds. After appearing on the balcony of Buckingham Palace with the King and Queen, he returned to Downing Street where he told the crowds that he had brought 'back from Germany peace with honour. I believe it is peace for our time'.

The aftermath of Munich

Reactions in Britain

Chamberlain received more than 40,000 letters of congratulation after his return from Munich, a number of them from Germans. He was also over-whelmed with gifts, from flowers to umbrellas and fishing rods. The press joined in the general feeling of relief that war had been averted. The Daily Express was typical, if a trifle overblown. 'Be glad in your hearts. Give thanks to God. The wings of peace settle about us and the peoples of Europe … People of Britain, your children are safe. Your husbands and your sons will not march to battle … The Prime Minister's conquests are mighty and enduring – millions of happy homes relieved of their burden.'

There was less euphoria in the Cabinet but only one resignation. Duff Cooper, the First Lord of the Admiralty, felt that the Munich terms were no real improvement on Hitler's Godesberg demands and that Chamberlain had put too much trust in Hitler's good faith. Other members of the Cabinet regarded the Munich agreement as a breathing space only, and wanted Britain's rearmament programme accelerated. Chamberlain disagreed. He feared that 'increases in the scope of our programme … would lead to a new arms race' and hoped that Munich would be the prelude to international discussion on the abolition of bombers.

The debate in the House of Commons gave Chamberlain's opponents a public platform. Churchill, predictably, denounced the Munich agreement as 'a total and unmitigated defeat'. He was supported by Clement Attlee, the leader of the Labour Party. The former Foreign Secretary, Anthony Eden, called for 'a national effort in the sphere of defence very much greater than anything than has been attempted hitherto'. As Chamberlain himself remarked: 'All the world seemed to be full of my praises except the House of Commons.' Nevertheless, support for the government was strong enough to ensure a majority of 222 at the end of the debate.

Hitler's reaction

Hitler was not pleased with the Munich agreement. He is reported to have remarked soon afterwards: 'That fellow Chamberlain has spoilt my entry into Prague.' He convinced himself that Britain and France would not have gone to war to defend Czechoslovakia and, on 21 October, secretly ordered his armed forces to be ready at any time to overrun the rest of the Czech state.

The change of mood in Britain

In the following months, the tone of Hitler's speeches, the Nazi propaganda machine and British Intelligence reports all suggested that Hitler's aggressive intentions had been encouraged rather than satisfied at Munich. A night of savage Nazi violence against Germany's Jewish community early in November shocked most German citizens and caused revulsion around the world. Public opinion in Britain hardened against Hitler's Germany. The government was defeated in two by-elections in November and Conservative Central Office became worried that the next general election might be lost. Chamberlain remained convinced that Anglo-German relations could be improved, but fewer of his colleagues agreed with him. The Foreign Secretary, Lord Halifax, took the lead in the Cabinet in urging a tougher policy towards Germany.

Chamberlain still hoped that Mussolini could be persuaded to prevent Hitler from carrying out what he called 'some mad dog act', but his visit with Halifax to Rome in January 1939 achieved little. Mussolini made it clear that he remained loyal to Germany. On 25 January Halifax warned the Cabinet that Hitler 'may be contemplating an attack on the West during the coming spring'. Chamberlain was not convinced, but he agreed that Britain would have to fight if Germany did attack in the west. This required a major change in Britain's strategy (see Chapter 3, page 19) and on 22 February the Cabinet agreed to prepare an army of eight divisions to fight in Europe.

The liquidation of Czechoslovakia

German troops entered Prague on 15 March. Hitler had spent the previous night bullying the new Czech president into inviting the Germans to invade. He had also told the Slovaks to declare themselves independent. This allowed the British government to evade the guarantee given to Czechoslovakia at Munich; they did not feel obliged to defend a state that no longer existed. But it was clear that Poland was likely to be Hitler's next target, and on 31 March Chamberlain announced to the House of Commons that if

Poland were attacked, Britain and France would 'lend the Polish Government all support in their power'.

The destruction of the Czech state made it clear that Hitler's ambitions went beyond the unity of all Germans. He had also displayed his contempt for the Munich agreement. Most people in Britain were now convinced that war with Germany was only a matter of time. Chamberlain, however, remained hopeful that peace could be secured. He recognised that he would have to take a tougher line with Germany and that rearmament would have to be accelerated but hoped that British firmness would bring Hitler to his senses and make him willing to negotiate. Chamberlain was reluctant to take steps likely to provoke Hitler into anything rash. This is why, for example, when he finally agreed in July to create a Ministry of Supply (to coordinate the production of munitions for war), he refused to appoint Churchill to the job, despite a strong press campaign, because doing so 'would certainly be regarded [by Hitler] as a challenge'.

The Polish crisis and the outbreak of war

German claims in Poland

Modern Poland, like Czechoslovakia, was created at the Paris peace conference of 1919. It had been granted a large strip of former German territory to provide access to the sea. Danzig, the port at the end of this Polish corridor, was overwhelmingly German in population but had been made a free city under League of Nations control. Ironically, the German claims against Poland, which Britain resisted, were more justified than those against Czechoslovakia, which Britain had accepted. Furthermore, Poland was not a democracy and had alienated British public opinion by seizing Teschen from Czechoslovakia at the time of Munich.

Hitler used Danzig in exactly the same way as he had the Sudetenland – as an excuse to force a crisis – although it is not clear at what stage he decided to conquer Poland rather than just make it into a satellite. The proximity of the USSR made it more of a problem for him than Czechoslovakia had been, but he was determined, after Munich, to ensure that Britain and France did not obstruct his plans. Chamberlain, as ever, thought that a peaceful solution was possible. As late as July he was writing to his sister: 'I can imagine that a way could be found of meeting German claims while safeguarding Poland's independence and economic security.'

The problem of the Russians

The Italians invaded Albania on 7 April, and Britain and France responded six days later with joint guarantees to Greece and Romania, thought to be imminent targets respectively of Italian and German aggression. When Chamberlain announced the guarantees to the House of Commons, his speech was interrupted by shouts of 'What about Russia?' Many MPs regarded an understanding with the USSR as vital if Britain's guarantees were to have any force. In June an opinion poll recorded 84% of the British public in favour of a military alliance between Britain, France and the USSR.

Chamberlain, though, did not want an alliance. The guarantees were designed to bring Hitler to the negotiating table, not form the basis of a hostile coalition. As the Chancellor of the Exchequer, Sir John Simon, put it in June: 'we are not preparing for war, we are constructing a peace front.' The British government regarded the Russians as untrustworthy, and sympathised with the Poles and Romanians when they refused to allow Soviet troops on to their territory. Chamberlain feared that a military alliance encircling Germany would provoke Hitler and make war more likely.

The military mission to Moscow

But Chamberlain could not ignore the Russians. Too many influential voices in Parliament and his own Cabinet believed that an agreement between the western democracies and the USSR was essential if Hitler were to be deterred from further aggression. Negotiations went on throughout the summer and, in early August, Britain and France sent a joint military mission to Moscow. Chamberlain was convinced that it would fail. 'We are only spinning out the time before the inevitable break comes,' he wrote. The decision to send the mission by sea meant that the talks began a full week after departure and emphasised Britain's lack of enthusiasm. One British general acidly suggested that they might as well have travelled by bicycle.

The Nazi–Soviet Pact

Once the talks got going, the main stumbling block was the refusal of the Poles and Romanians to allow Soviet troops to cross their territory. Without such an agreement, a treaty with the USSR was worthless. As the negotiations stalled, Hitler seized his opportunity. On 23 August the Nazi Foreign Minister, Ribbentrop, arrived in Moscow and, in the early hours of the following morning, signed a ten-year non-aggression pact with Stalin. An additional secret protocol divided eastern Europe into German and Soviet spheres of influence.

The outbreak of war

Hitler hoped that, with all chance of Russian help gone, Britain and France would abandon Poland to her fate. Instead, Chamberlain responded by making the Polish guarantee into a more formal treaty on 25 August. The Germans attacked Poland on 1 September but the British government did not declare war immediately. Chamberlain still had faint hopes of a negotiated settlement. When he met the House of Commons on 2 September there was uproar because MPs feared that another Munich was in the offing. Even Chamberlain's supporters were angry. There was a similar revolt in the Cabinet for the same reason. Britain and France finally declared war on Germany on Sunday 3 September.

Why did Britain go to war in 1939?

The phoney war

In one sense Britain did not go to war in 1939. The guarantee to Poland had been a bluff, designed to frighten Hitler, not defend Poland. As Hitler realised, there was little that Britain could do to help, and the French were determined to remain on the defensive in the west. A period known as 'the phoney war' lasted until April 1940 when the Germans invaded Denmark and Norway. Chamberlain wanted to prevent the carnage of a major war and hoped that German economic difficulties, worsened by a British naval blockade, would cause the downfall of the Nazi regime and make a negotiated peace possible. He clung to a faint hope that appeasement might yet triumph.

Britain's status and security

Yet British leaders also realised that, as in 1914, neither Britain nor France could remain great powers if they allowed Hitler a completely free hand in Europe. The Versailles Settlement of 1919, however flawed, represented the triumph of the western democracies over the Germans' previous attempt to dominate Europe. British politicians were prepared to allow the Germans to tinker with the Versailles terms, but not dismantle them altogether. By 1939 it was plain that Hitler intended to destroy, not just amend, the Versailles Settlement. In this sense, Britain and France went to war in 1939 to defend the map of Europe which they themselves had drawn up in 1919.

Furthermore, as Halifax put it in a speech in June 1939, 'we know that, if the security and independence of other countries are to disappear, our own security and our own independence will be gravely threatened'. The events of 1940 demonstrated all too clearly how vulnerable Britain was once France and the Low Countries had fallen.

Studying Chamberlain and appeasement

1   At what point do you think Chamberlain should have abandoned his attempt to reach a lasting agreement with Hitler? Consider each of the following in turn and list the reasons why he should, or should not, have given up at that point:
- When he became Prime Minister
- After the *Anschluss*
- After the Weekend Crisis
- After Godesberg
- After Munich
- After the German invasion of Czechoslovakia.

Remember to consider what advice he was getting at each stage from Cabinet colleagues, his French allies, service chiefs, the intelligence community and his diplomats abroad. Think about the state of public opinion, the views of MPs and what he knew about Britain's economic and military capability, German power and the number of British allies he had.

2   Chamberlain did not want a Russian alliance in 1939. Was he right? List your reasons for supporting or opposing him.

6 *Historical interpretations*

Key themes

◆ Churchill and the Guilty Men
◆ The post-war political consensus
◆ A. J. P. Taylor and the Origins of the Second World War
◆ Revisionism
◆ The historical reputations of Churchill and Chamberlain

Churchill and the Guilty Men

When the British Army staggered back to Dunkirk in May 1940, battered and demoralised after barely a month's fighting, the nation had suffered one of the most humiliating defeats in its history. Three left-wing journalists (one of whom, Michael Foot, was to become leader of the Labour Party in the early 1980s) immediately published a short book under the pseudonym 'Cato'. Called *Guilty Men*, it blamed the defeat on the politicians of the 1930s for their 'criminal' complacency and short-sightedness in failing to rearm the nation in the face of the threat from Germany. The book helped to create the popular myth that appeasement had been a policy of foolish and craven submission to brute force.

The defeat of Germany in 1945 revealed for the first time the full horrors of the Nazi policies of persecution and mass murder. Shocking pictures of the emaciated survivors of Belsen and Auschwitz caused revulsion in the western world, not only for Hitler's regime, but also for the French and British politicians of the 1930s who had been prepared to trust the German dictator.

In 1948 Winston Churchill published *The Gathering Storm*, the first volume in his Second World War memoirs. As the Prime Minister whose resolute leadership, especially in the dark days of 1940, had stiffened national morale and contributed to victory in 1945, Churchill was already firmly established as one of the great heroes of British history, and his verdict on appeasement was bound to be hugely influential. In 600 pages he endorsed the judgements made by the authors of *Guilty Men*: Baldwin had failed to rearm because he feared electoral defeat, Chamberlain had been duped by Hitler, only Churchill and a courageous few had warned of the perils. Within two years nearly 500,000 copies of the book had been sold in Britain and the United States, and Churchill's influence on the history of appeasement was firmly established. It has never since been fully dislodged.

The post-war political consensus

For about 30 years after the Second World War the economic ideas of the 1930s were as unfashionable as appeasement. The War had seemed to demonstrate, and both major political parties accepted, that unemployment could be banished if the government played an active part in managing the economy. This made the Treasury of the 1930s, which had insisted that little could be done about unemployment and that the nation could only afford to rearm slowly, appear as timid and cowardly as the diplomats and politicians.

Britain remained a major imperial power until the 1960s, and Britain's role as the one of the world's 'great powers' was accepted by both Conservative and Labour politicians. Few challenged the notion that Britain continued to have an important part to play in the Cold War against the USSR. In this context, it was thought important to avoid the mistakes of the 1930s. The potentially expansionist and aggressive designs of the Soviet Union should be resisted, not appeased. Anthony Eden, Britain's premier in 1956, justified his invasion of Egypt partly by comparing Nasser's nationalisation of the Suez Canal with Hitler's march into the Rhineland in 1936.

A.J.P. Taylor and the Origins of the Second World War

Published in 1961, A. J. P. Taylor's book *The Origins of the Second World War* had a major impact on the debate surrounding the outbreak of what, until then, had been regarded simply as Hitler's war. Taylor's thesis was that Hitler's foreign policy was essentially no different from that of other German leaders. He merely wanted to make Germany the strongest power in Europe. The war had come about because Britain and France, by falling over themselves to appease him, had given him his opportunity. 'The Fascist dictators would not have gone to war unless they had seen a chance of winning,' wrote Taylor. 'The cause of war was therefore as much the blunders of others as the wickedness of the dictators themselves.'

Taylor's book was immediately controversial but only because of what he said about Hitler, not because of his criticisms of Britain and France. These were endorsed in 1963 by Martin Gilbert and Richard Gott in their indictment of Chamberlain called *The Appeasers*. They concluded that Chamberlain and his advisers had been 'ruthless and unprincipled' in their pursuit of the appeasement of Germany. They had deceived the public and risked 'dishonour and humiliation' in their pursuit of peace at any price. After almost a quarter of a century, the verdict of the authors of *Guilty Men* still held sway.

Revisionism

By the 1970s and 1980s, not only were the Cabinet minutes and government papers of the 1930s open for scrutiny, but the economic ideas of that decade had come back into fashion. A wealth of historical study examined the context in which the politicians of the 1930s had operated, and emphasised the difficulties and constraints afflicting Chamberlain and his colleagues. Michael Howard's brilliant little book, *The Continental Commitment* (1972), demonstrated the problems that Britain faced in the 1930s when defending her vast Empire, and showed how divided the service chiefs were about strategic priorities. In 1979 G.C. Peden published *British Rearmament and the Treasury 1932–1939*, which argued that Treasury concerns about the ability of the British economy both to rearm the forces in the short term and to maintain supplies in a long war were generally well founded. Paul Kennedy's *The Realities behind Diplomacy* (1981) drew together the work of a number of historians in analysing the range of domestic pressures that helped to shape appeasement policies.

The historical reputations of Churchill and Chamberlain

In 1989 John Charmley published *Chamberlain and the Lost Peace*, and followed it in 1993 with *Churchill, the End of Glory*. He completed his trilogy in 1995 with *Churchill's Grand Alliance*. Charmley believes that Chamberlain's policy was the only realistic course open to Britain because another major war could only destroy her power and influence in the world. For Charmley, Churchill was an old-fashioned romantic whose dogged defence of the British Empire in the Second World War served only to replace British influence with American. Furthermore, the war handed eastern Europe over to Stalin, whose dictatorship was no better than that of Hitler. For Charmley, the authors of *Guilty Men* could not have been more wrong; Chamberlain was the clear-eyed, courageous realist and Churchill the deluded optimist.

But there remain plenty of modern historians ready to defend Churchill and criticise Chamberlain. Richard Cockett's 1989 study *Twilight of Truth* demonstrates the lengths to which Chamberlain went to ensure that the press supported his policies and how successful he was in gaining press backing. Andrew Roberts, in his 1991 biography of the Foreign Secretary Lord Halifax, demonstrated Chamberlain's isolation in 1939 by showing the extent to which Halifax disagreed with appeasement after Munich. Alistair Parker's *Chamberlain and Appeasement* (1993) argues that Chamberlain chose appeasement of Germany because he believed in it; financial constraints, domestic pressures and strategic difficulties merely reinforced his convictions. He also maintains that Chamberlain stuck to the policy long after it was evident to everyone else that Hitler could not be trusted and, as a result, viable alternatives to appeasement were never tried.

Further reading

Of the books mentioned above, *Guilty Men* (1940) is written with great panache. Churchill's *The Gathering Storm* (1948) and Taylor's *The Origins of the Second World War* (1961) should be approached with caution because both authors, though brilliant, have axes to grind. Michael Howard, *The Continental Commitment* (1972), and Paul Kennedy, *The Realities behind Diplomacy* (1981), are both essential and immensely readable. John Charmley, *Chamberlain and the Lost Peace* (1989) and Alistair Parker, *Chamberlain and Appeasement* (1993) are detailed and scholarly. In addition to these, *Retreat from Power* (Volume 1) (1981), edited by David Dilks, contains a number of important essays on aspects of appeasement. David Reynolds, *Britannia Overruled* (1991), and C. J. Bartlett, *British Foreign Policy in the Twentieth Century* (1989), provide stimulating assessments of Britain's relative decline as a world power.

Timeline

1919	Versailles Peace Conference		**1938**	
	Ten Year Rule introduced		12 Mar	German invasion of Austria
1920	League of Nations inaugurated		21–22 May	'Weekend Crisis' over rumours of
1921	Washington Naval Treaty			German mobilisation against
1922	Irish Free State granted dominion status			Czechoslovakia
1923	French invasion of the Ruhr		4 Aug – 15 Sept	Runciman mission to
1925	Locarno Treaties			Czechoslovakia
1928	Ten Year Rule extended		12 Sept	Hitler's speech on Czech crisis at
1929	Wall Street Crash			Nuremberg Party Rally
1930	London Naval Conference		15 Sept	Hitler's first meeting with
1931	Statute of Westminster makes the Dominions			Chamberlain at Berchtesgaden
	fully independent		18 Sept	Anglo-French talks in London:
	Major economic crisis drives the Labour			transfer of Sudetenland agreed
	Government from office		22–23 Sept	Hitler's second meeting with
	National Government formed			Chamberlain at Godesberg
	Mukden incident: start of Japanese invasion of		25 Sept	British Cabinet rejects Godesberg
	Manchuria			demands
1932	Shanghai crisis		29–30 Sept	Munich Conference and
	Disarmament Conference opens in Geneva			Agreement
	Ten Year Rule abandoned		21 Oct	Wehrmacht ordered to prepare for
1933	Hitler appointed Chancellor of Germany			invasion of rest of Czechoslovakia
	Defence Requirements Committee formed		**1939**	
	Fulham by-election		22 Feb	British government decides to
1934	First report of the Defence Requirements			prepare army for continental war
	Committee		15 Mar	German occupation of Bohemia
1935	Hitler announces existence of German *Luftwaffe*			and Moravia
	and reintroduction of conscription		31 Mar	Anglo-French guarantee to Poland
	Stresa Agreements between Britain, France and		7 Apr	Italian invasion of Albania
	Italy		13 Apr	Anglo-French guarantees to
	Anglo-German Naval Agreement			Romania and Greece
	Italian invasion of Abyssinia		27 Apr	Introduction of conscription in
	Hoare-Laval Pact			Britain
1936	German remilitarisation of the Rhineland		12 Aug	Anglo-French military mission
	Fall of Addis Ababa to the Italians			begins talks in Moscow
	Outbreak of Spanish Civil War		24 Aug	German-Soviet Non-Aggression
1937	Neville Chamberlain becomes British Prime			Pact signed in Moscow
	Minister		25 Aug	Anglo-Polish treaty signed
	Sino-Japanese war begins		1 Sept	German invasion of Poland
	Halifax's meeting with Hitler		3 Sept	British and French declarations of
	Inskip Report			war on Germany

Table 1: Percentage shares of world manufacturing output

	1860	1880	1900	1913	1928	1938
UK	19.9	22.9	18.5	13.6	9.9	10.7
Germany	4.9	8.5	13.2	14.8	11.6	12.7
Russia	7.0	7.6	8.8	8.2	5.3	9.0
USA	7.2	14.7	23.6	32.0	39.3	31.4
Japan	2.6	2.4	2.4	2.7	3.3	5.2

Table 2: German air strength and British estimates of it, 1938

	German strength, Aug 1938		British estimates, Sept 1938	
	Total	Combat ready	Total	Combat ready
Fighters	643	453	810	717
Bombers	1,157	582	1,235	1,019
Dive-bombers	207	159	247	227

Table 3: Allied and German air strength, Sept 1938 and Sept 1939

	Sept 1938			Sept 1939		
	A	B	C	A	B	C
Germany	2,847	1,669	–	3,609	2,893	900
Britain	1,982	1,642	412	1,911	1,600	2,200
France	1,454	–	730	1,792	–	1,600

A: First-line strength, B: Serviceable first-line aircraft, C: Reserves

Table 4: Government Social Services expenditure in £ millions

Year	Expenditure	Contributions	% met by contributions
1913–14	41.5	19.0	45.8
1921–22	234.0	55.5	23.7
1933–34	292.0	88.5	30.3

Principal Personalities

	Prime Minister
1931–35	Ramsay MacDonald
1935–37	Stanley Baldwin
1937–40	Neville Chamberlain

	Foreign Secretary
1931–35	Sir John Simon
1935	Sir Samuel Hoare
1935–38	Anthony Eden
1938–40	Lord Halifax

	Chancellor of the Exchequer
1931–37	Neville Chamberlain
1937–40	Sir John Simon